THE ILLUSTRATED BIBLE ATLAS

WITH HISTORICAL NOTES BY F.F. BRUCE

De La Salle House

Carta, Jerusalem
Distributed by

TABLE OF CONTENTS

Foreword 3
Ancient Near East in the
   Second Millennium B.C. 4
     Palace at Mari 4
The Near East in the First Millennium B.C. 6
     Babylon 6

The Old Testament
The Exodus 8
The Coming of the Israelites 9
     The Walls of Jericho 9
Jerusalem at the Time of David and Solomon .. 10
Solomon's Temple 10
The Kingdom of David and Solomon 11
     Megiddo – Chariot City 11
The Kingdoms of Judah and Israel 13
     The Palace at Samaria 13

The Hellenistic World
The World of the Greeks 14
     Empire of Alexander the Great 14
Palestine in Graeco-Roman Times 17
     Jerusalem of the Hasmoneans 17

The Roman Empire 18
     Rome 18

The New Testament
The Temple at the Time of Jesus 20
Jerusalem at the Time of Jesus 20
Jesus in His Land 21
     Qumran of the Essenes 21
The Journeys of the Apostles 23
     Antioch 23
     Caesarea Maritima 23
The Spread of the Early Church 24
Paul's First and Second Missionary Journeys ... 25
Paul's Third Missionary Journey
   and Trip to Rome 25
The Growth of Christianity 27

Modern Times
The Near East – Physical 28
Modern Israel 28
Modern Jerusalem 29
Chronological Table 30
Index to Maps 31

The Illustrated Bible Atlas

Copyright © 1994 by Carta, The Israel Map and Publishing Company, Ltd., Jerusalem

Distributed by Kregel Publications, a division of Kregel, Inc., P.O. Box 2607, Grand Rapids, MI 49501. Kregel Publications provides trusted, biblical publications for Christian growth and service. Your comments and suggestions are valued.

All rights reserved. No part of this book may be reproduced, stored in a retrieval system, or transmitted in any form or by any means—electronic, mechanical, photocopy, recording, or otherwise—without written permission of the publisher, except for brief quotations in printed reviews.

For more information about Kregel Publications, visit our web site at http://www.kregel.com.

ISBN 0-8254-2086-5

Printed in Israel

1 2 3 4 / 02 01 00 99 98

FOREWORD

This Atlas is designed as an aid to the study of the Bible. The contents of the Bible are so closely related to the lands or cities in which the recorded events took place and in which the documents themselves were written that it helps greatly to know something about those lands and cities. This is one kind of knowledge that the Atlas provides.

Moreover, the writing of the books of the Bible spans a period of some 1,400 years, and the history which they record reaches back to the beginnings of civilization in the ancient Near East. To understand them properly, it is necessary to have some knowledge of the historical as well as the geographical setting. The maps are arranged in historical sequence, and the notes to the maps are intended to relate the Bible story to its historical background.

A further and very useful aid is supplied by the chronological table on page 30.

F. F. Bruce

Hammurabi

The second millennium B.C. was a great imperial age in the ancient Near East. In the Euphrates-Tigris valley, the Assyrian and Babylonian empires enjoyed periods of expansion with alternating periods of weakness. On the Middle Euphrates, the kingdom of Mari (18th century B.C.) extended its authority into Syria. Later, the kingdom of Mitanni flourished in the Upper Euphrates valley: its ruler was sufficiently important to correspond with the King of Egypt as an equal. The two dominant empires for most of the millennium, however, were those of the Egyptians and the Hittites.

The Egyptians enjoyed two periods of power – the Middle Kingdom (Dynasty XII) from about 1991 to 1786 B.C., and the New Kingdom (Dynasties XVIII and XIX) from about 1560 to 1200 B.C. Between these two phases, Egypt was invaded and dominated by Semites from Asia, known as the Hyksos.

The kingdom of the Hittites, established in Asia Minor soon after 2000 B.C., became an imperial power and extended its rule south into Syria, reaching its zenith under Suppiluliumas (c. 1380–1350

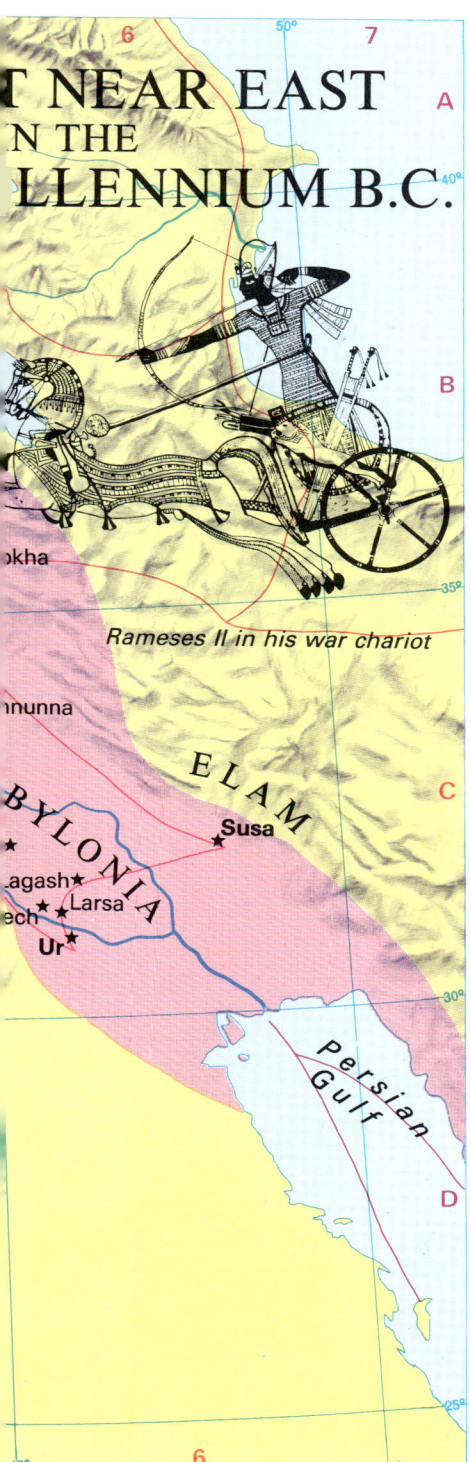

Egyptian warship, 1200 B.C.

Thutmose III

B.C.). As the Egyptian rulers of Dynasty XVIII extended their power northward, they came into contact with the Hittites, their relations being sometimes diplomatic and sometimes hostile. A battle was fought between the two empires in 1286 B.C. at Kedesh on the Orontes in Syria; it was followed by a treaty confirming the Orontes as the frontier between the spheres of interest. The treaty was cemented by the marriage of a Hittite princess to the Egyptian king Rameses II (of Dynasty XIX).

About 1200 B.C. the Hittite empire collapsed and Egypt began to enter a further period of decline.

In this context are to be set the movements of the Hebrew patriarchs recorded in Genesis and Exodus. Abraham left Ur in southern Mesopotamia and settled for a time in Harran, east of the Upper Euphrates; then he moved on to Caanan, where he lived as a pastoral nomad. Once, because of a famine, he paid a short visit to Egypt. His descendants maintained their links with Harran for two generations. Many of them, in a time of prolonged famine, went down from Canaan to Egypt and settled there for four generations. Their departure from Egypt under Moses and their settlement in Canaan under Joshua (c. 1200 B.C.) marked the beginning of Israel's history as a nation.

THE NEAR EAST IN THE FIRST MILLENNIUM B.C.

Legend:
- Greatest extent of Assyrian Empire, early 7th cent. B.C.
- Neo-Babylonian Empire
- Egypt
- Phrygians
- Major route

BABYLON (6th century B.C.)

Assyrian battle chariot

The first millennium B.C. witnessed a recession in the power of Egypt. Occasionally a powerful king would attempt to reassert Egyptian authority in Canaan. Shishak, for example (of Dynasty XXII), invaded the kingdoms of Judah and Israel in about 925 B.C.: one account of his invasion is given in Kings 14:25-28 and another, Shishak's own record, appears in relief on the walls of the temple of Amun at Karnak (Thebes). But he did not maintain control over the territory he invaded.

Between 1000 and 612 B.C., the dominant power in the Near East was Assyria. In 852 B.C. a concerted effort was made by the states of Cilicia and Syria (including Israel) to halt the Assyrians' westward advance. They gave battle to the Assyrians at Qarqar on the Orontes, and its was twelve years before the Assyrians returned. But when they did return, they proved irresistible. One after another the western kingdoms fell before them: Damascus in 732 B.C., Israel (Samaria) in 721 B.C., while Judah survived as a weak vassal state. At the height of its power, the Assyrian Empire extended over Elam (east of the Persian Gulf), Armenia, southeast Asia Minor, Syria and Palestine, and for a short time Egypt itself. Thebes, capital of upper Egypt, was sacked in 663 B.C.

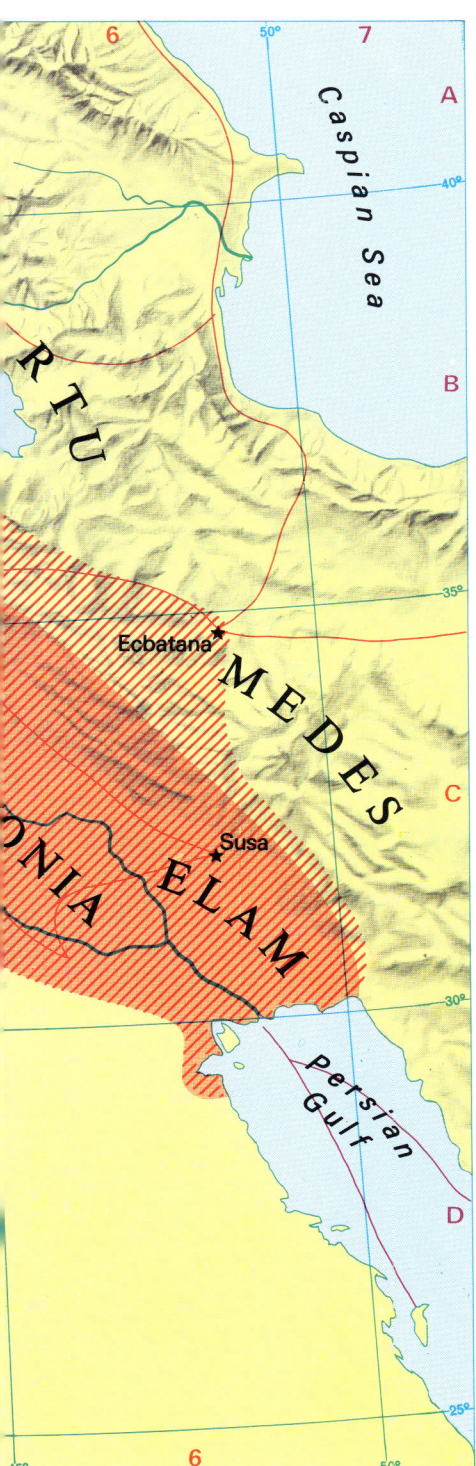

Phoenician merchant ship, 7th century B.C.

A Median leading horses

    But Assyria was overthrown at last by the Medes from the east and the Babylonians from the south; they divided among themselves the former Assyrian territory. Nineveh fell in 612 B.C. The Egyptians, trying to gain some advantage for themselves from this new turn of events, were defeated in 605 B.C. at Carchemish on the Euphrates by the Babylonians, who established control as far as the frontier of Egypt.

    The Median kingdom lasted for 63 years after the fall of Nineveh; then it fell in its turn before Cyrus, ruler of a small kingdom on the Persian Gulf and founder of the Persian Empire. In a few years Cyrus, having secured sovereignty over the dual monarchy of the Medes and Persians, pushed his empire west to the Aegean Sea. Then he captured Babylon in 539 B.C. He is commemorated in the Bible for his edict authorizing the return of the Jews who had been exiled from their homeland by the Babylonians. His son Cambyses conquered Egypt in 525 B.C.. The Persian empire stood for 200 years, stretching "from India to Ethiopia" (Esther 1:1); it was finally overthrown by Alexander the Great (331 B.C.).

Rameses II

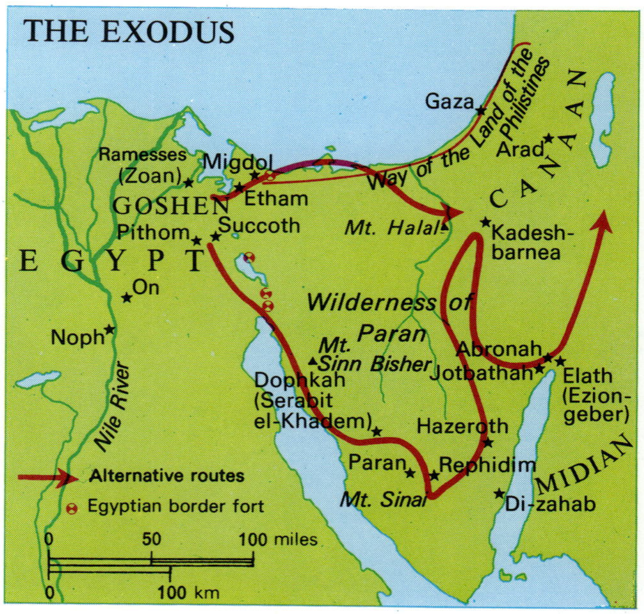

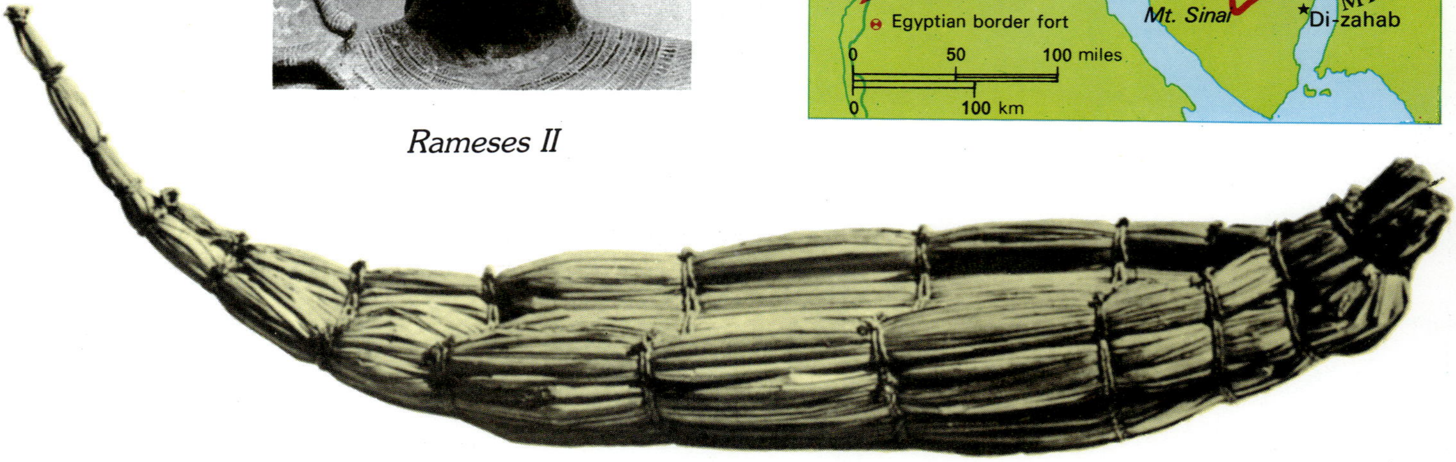

Egyptian reed boat

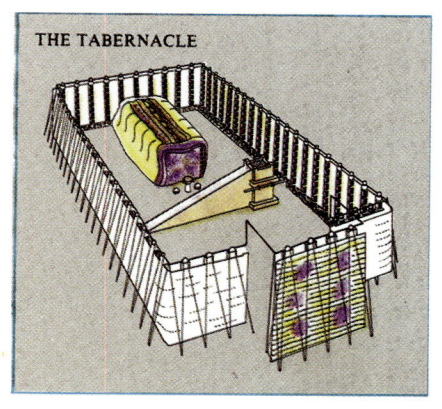

Model of the Tabernacle

The main body of the Israelites that left Egypt under Moses moved east through the Wilderness of Zin and then north through Transjordan. Those who advanced northwest from Kadesh-Barnea into the Negev did not necessarily turn back, as might be inferred from the map; after the defeat of the King of Arad at Hormah (Numbers 21:1-3), some members of the tribe of Judah and their local allies probably consolidated their position and penetrated farther, in the direction of Hebron.

Turning west from Transjordan, the main body crossed the Jordan opposite Jericho. After capturing that citadel, they penetrated into the central highlands, from which some turned north to the Plain of Jezreel and others turned southwest, defeating a coalition of Canaanite kings at the battle of Beth-horon. A minor branch of that body that entered Transjordan advanced north instead of crossing the Jordan and occupied the Amorite territories south and north of the Jabbok.

The areas of settlement did not include the plains, which the Canaanite city-states continued to dominate with their iron reinforced chariotry. The power of the Canaanites in the Plain of Jezreel was weakened by an Israelite victory won at the river Kishon in c. 1125 B.C. But the Israelites were continually menaced by bedouin from the east and, more seriously, by Philistines from the western seaboard. The Philistines, who were refugees from the Aegean area, gradually extended their control over most of the land west of the Jordan.

For most of this period the tribes of Israel were too disunited to take effective action against their enemies. Their central sanctuary at Shiloh, in Ephraimite territory, housed the Ark of the Covenant, the symbol of their religious unity, but its role as a cohesive influence was limited. The "judges" who gave their name to the Book of Judges, which deals with the two centuries between the Israelites' early settlement and the rise of the monarchy, exercised authority for the most part over limited areas.

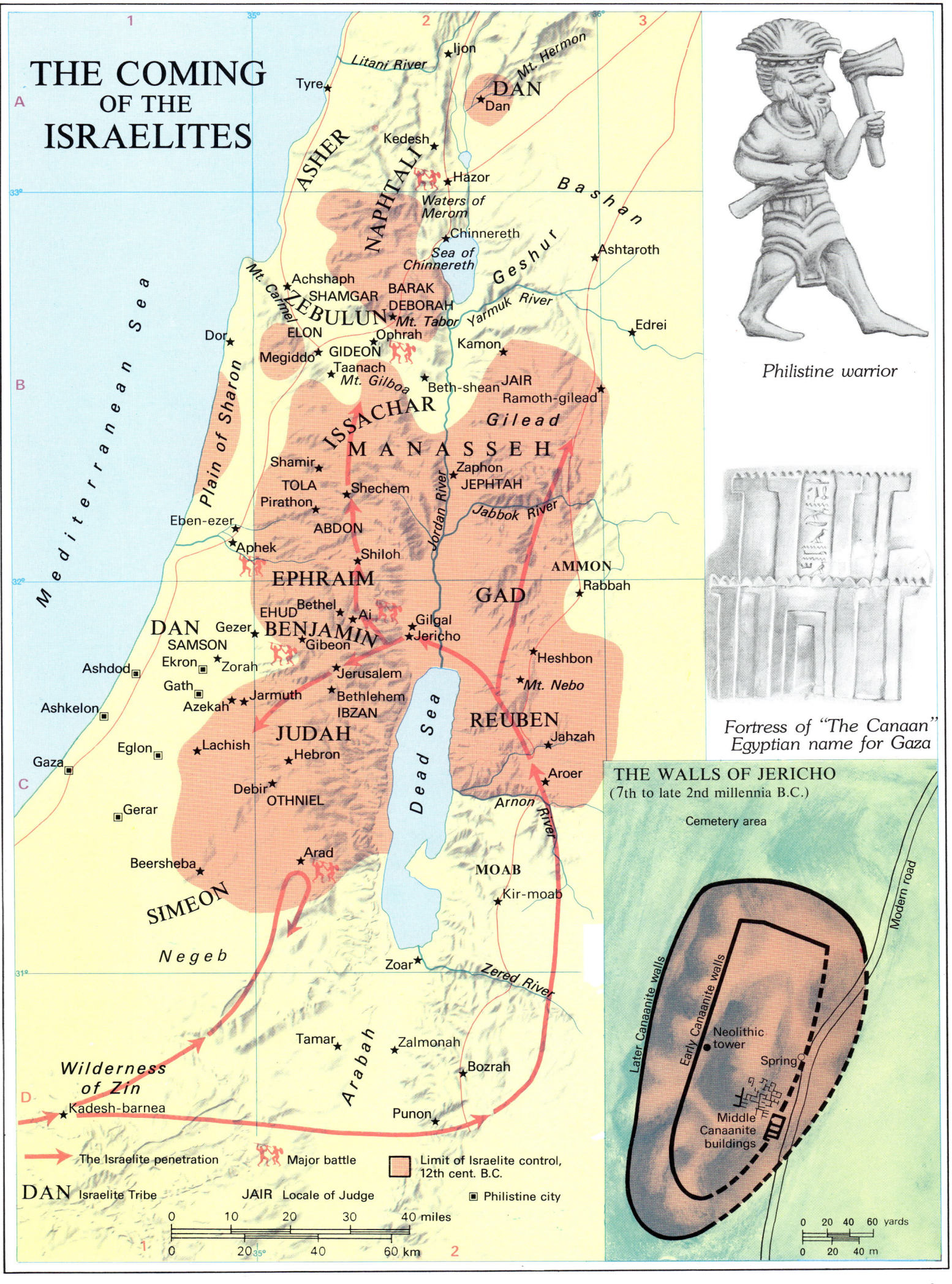

The Philistine menace moved the Israelites to choose a king, a military leader for their whole federation. Their choice fell on Saul, a man from the tribe of Benjamin, who gave early promise of deserving their confidence. But in an attempt to restore communications between the central tribes and those in the north, who were cut off from their fellow-Israelites by the Philistine occupation of the Plain of Jezreel, Saul was killed at the battle of Mount Gilboa (c. 1010 B.C.). The Philistines now controlled all Canaan west of the Jordan.

The preservation of Israel's national identity was due to David, a Judaean from Bethlehem, who with his guerrilla force had been for some time in the service of one of the Philistine rulers. With Philistine permission he was installed as king of Judah. When, two years later, Saul's last surviving son was assassinated, all the tribes of Israel invited David to be their king. At first the Philistines raised no objection, thinking that he was still their vassal. But when he strengthened his position by the sudden capture of Jerusalem, which had remained a Canaanite city until now, the Philistines realized that he would threaten their supremacy if he were not immediately crushed. After defeating them in two battles, however, it was David who reduced the Philistines to subjection. Then, by conquest and alliance, he extended his rule until his sphere of influence included all Transjordan and stretched north to the Euphrates.

He bequeathed this minor empire to his son Solomon (c. 970-930 B.C.), whose desire to imitate the style of a great king in his capital at Jerusalem imposed on his people a burden too heavy to bear. By the time of his death most of Israel's subject-nations had regained their independence, and soon after his death his own kingdom split into two parts – the kingdom of Israel in the north and central Canaan and the kingdom of Judah in the south, retaining Jerusalem as its capital.

The "Sea" of cast metal

JERUSALEM AT THE TIME OF DAVID AND SOLOMON

SOLOMON'S TEMPLE

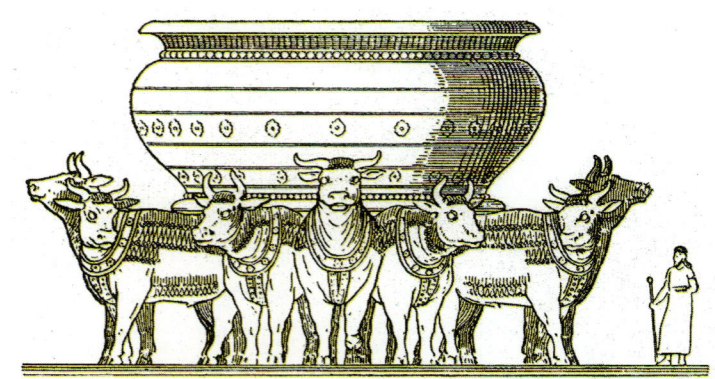

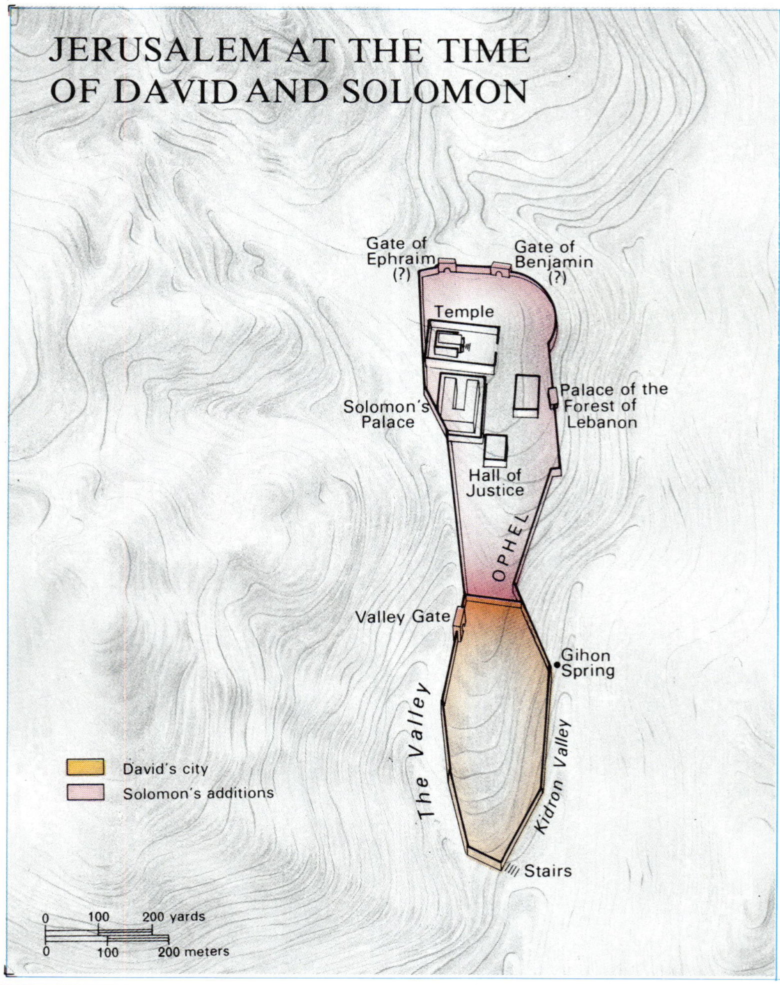

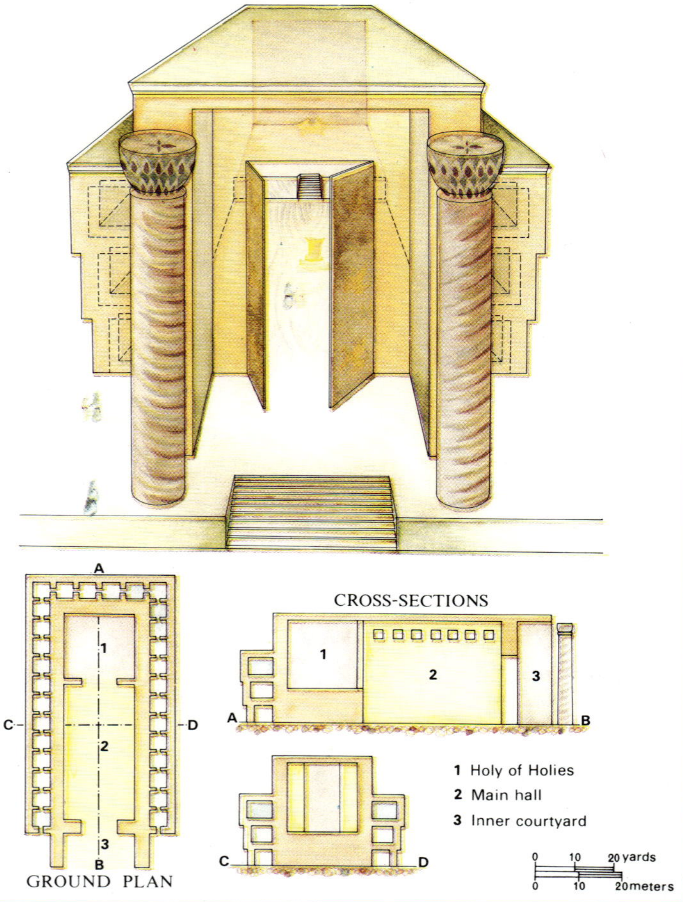

Assryian army attacks a city, palace of Tiglath-Pileser III, Calah

The united kingdom of David and Solomon was inevitably weakened by being divided. Almost immediately after the division, both of the succession kingdoms were further weakened by the invasion of the Egyptians under Shishak. Moreover, the two kingdoms waged war with each other for half a century: the dynasty of David in the south did not readily abandon the hope of bringing the northern kingdom back under its control.

In the north, one upstart dynasty after another seized power with disconcerting frequency. The strongest of the northern dynasties was founded by Omri, who built a new strategic capital at Samaria (c. 880 B.C.). Under Omri and his successors, Israel and Judah were at peace with each other. Judah regained control over Edom, with access to the Gulf of Aqaba; Israel reduced the Transjordanian Moabites to servitude. Israel's great enemy at this time was the Aramaean kingdom of Damascus. But for a year or two even the king of Damascus had to make common cause with Israel (under Omri's son Ahab) to resist the incursion of Shalmaneser III of Assyria; they contributed major contingents to the united army which halted his advance in 853 B.C.

With the fall of the dynasty of Omri (841 B.C.), Israel's position against the Aramaeans was weakened; it seemed at one stage as if they would wipe Israel out. But the damage caused to Damascus by an Assyrian raid in 803 B.C. gave Israel a respite. For the next forty or fifty years both Israel and Judah enjoyed renewed prosperity under Jeroboam II in the north and Uzziah in the south.

This prosperity was brought to an end by fresh attacks from Assyria, which from 745 B.C. onward established its empire over south-western Asia. The kingdoms of Damascus and Samaria were abolished and replaced by Assyrian provinces; the kingdom of Judah escaped a similar fate by the skin of its teeth. The recession of Assyrian power from 625 B.C. onward enabled Josiah, king of Judah, to assert his independence and reform the national religion. But this independence was shortlived. With the fall of Assyria, Babylon became the dominant power in those regions. Had Judah been content to remain tributary to Babylon, it might have survived; as it was, it revolted against Babylon at the instigation of Egypt. In reprisal, the Babylonians destroyed Jerusalem and its temple and deported large numbers of the Judaean population to the east (587 B.C.).

The Mesha Stele

THE WORLD OF THE GREEKS

Alexander the Great

EMPIRE OF ALEXANDER THE GREAT
(late 4th century B.C.)

- ▨ Former Persian Empire
- ▰ Alexander's Empire
- → Routes taken by Alexander's army
- ■ Cities founded by Alexander

- ▰ Greek sphere
- ▨ Phoenician-Punic sphere
- ▰ Rome c.300 B.C.
- ⋯ Boundary of Persian Empire, c.350 B.C.
- — Major sea route

Alexander the Great in battle

Greek merchant ship, 6th century B.C.

Seleucus I

As far back as historical records go, the Greeks lived in city states on the Greek mainland and islands. Three waves of migration into Greece have been envisaged: (1) the Ionians, (2) the Achaeans (with the Aeolians), and (3) the Dorians. The Dorian migration from the North (c. 1000 B.C.) is the only one to have survived in historical memory. Pressed by later migrants, the earlier settlers crossed the Aegean and settled on the west coast of Asia Minor. Prominent among these were the Ionians: it was by their name that the Greeks were known in Western Asia. The Old Testament name Javan (Hebrew – *yawan*) is identical with Ion. From the Aegean world, Greek colonists sailed farther afield to the shores of the Black Sea, Sicily and South Italy (which was called Magna Graecia, "Great Greece") and southeastern France (including Marseilles and the lower Rhone Valley).

The Greek city-states made common cause in resisting the Persian invasions under Darius I (490 B.C.) and his son Xerxes (480 B.C.). But in general they remained divided and often at war with one another until they were conquered one by one by Philip II of Macedonia (356-336 B.C.) and incorporated in his Graeco-Macedonian empire. Philip's son Alexander the Great (336-323 B.C.) embarked on a campaign of conquest which carried him up the Nile and east through Afghanistan to the Indus valley. The Persian Empire disintegrated before his advance, but Alexander's united empire which took its place did not outlive him. After his death his leading generals divided it among themselves. Of the succession kingdoms the two which figure most in Biblical history were the kingdom of Ptolemy and his successors in Egypt (ruling from Alexander's city of Alexandria) and that of Seleucus and his successors in Western Asia (ruling from Antioch in Syria). The Jews were now under Greek instead of Persian sovereignty. Until 198 B.C. they were subject to the Ptolemies; then, after a defeat inflicted on the Ptolemaic army by Antiochus III, they were subject for over fifty years to the Seleucids.

Even if Alexander's empire did not retain its political unity, it established a cultural unity. The Greek language and way of life were carried through the whole area of Alexander's conquests. Judaea was not immune to this hellenizing influence, but those Jews who settled in large numbers in Alexandria, Antioch and other Greek cities, were thoroughly hellenized. They continued to worship the God of Israel, but their synagogue services were conducted in Greek, and for their benefit – in the first instance, for the benefit of Alexandrian Jews – their scriptures were translated from Hebrew into Greek. This is the translation commonly called the Septuagint.

Antiochus III

The Emperor Augustus

Palestine is a shortened form of the name given to the country by the Greeks and Romans: *Syria Palaestina*. It perpetuates the name of the Philistines, one of the many elements in its earlier population. It was subject to the Persians until 332 B.C. Then it was incorporated in the empire of Alexander the Great, who set up governors in Samaria and Judaea. After Alexander's death (323 B.C), Palestine became a bone of contention between the Ptolemies in Egypt and the Seleucids in Syria. The Ptolemies held it until 198 B.C.; in that year Antiochus III of Syria defeated Ptolemy V at Panion (modern Banyas), one of the sources of the Jordan, and wrested Palestine from him.

Under the Ptolemies and Seleucids Palestine was hellenized, largely by the founding of several Greek cities on the Mediterranean seaboard and in the Jordan valley. The latter included ten cities of the Decapolis (cf. Matthew 4:25; Mark 5:20; 7:31). Even the Aramaic-speaking areas were much influenced by Greek language and culture.

The taxation of the territory was managed by an efficient bureaucracy and proved burdensome to the inhabitants, especially when Antiochus III, after his defeat by the Romans at Magnesia, had to raise money to pay the crushing indemnity they imposed on him. His son, Antiochus IV (175-163 B.C.), suspecting the Judaeans of disloyalty to his dynasty, deprived them of their inherited privileges and even banned the practice of their religion. This precipitated a revolt, led by Judas Maccabeus and his brothers, members of the Hasmonaean priestly family. Judas was a gifted guerrilla leader, and won a series of victories which led, at the end of 164 B.C., to the restoration of religious freedom and the rededication of the Jerusalem temple to the worship of the God of Israel. Twenty-two years later, the restoration of religious freedom was followed by the regaining of political freedom, and for seventy-nine years the independent Jewish state was governed by the Hasmonaean dynasty.

When the Roman general Pompey, reorganizing Western Asia after putting down Mithridates, king of Pontus, arrived in Syria, he was invited to intervene in a feud between two princes of the Hasmonaean family. His intervention meant the end of Jewish independence. He occupied the city and temple of Jerusalem in 63 B.C.

Under the Romans an Idumaean statesman, Antipater, and his son Herod increased their power in Judaea. They made themselves so indispensable to the Romans that at last the Roman senate conferred on Herod the title of king of the Jews. His reign (37-4 B.C.) proved oppressive to his subjects, but he maintained peace and retained the confidence of his Roman master. He was a great builder. He founded Sebaste on the site of the ancient Samaria, and constructed a great harbor-city at Caesaria on the Mediterranean Sea. His best-known building achievement was the restoration and enlargement of the temple in Jerusalem.

At his death in 4 B.C., the Emperor Augustus divided Herod's kingdom among three of his sons. Judaea (with Samaria) went to Archelaus, Galilee and Peraea to Antipas, and the territory east and northeast of the lake of Galilee to Philip. Philip and Antipas ruled their territories for many years, but Archelaus's subjects found his rule so harsh that Augustus deposed him in A.D. 6, and Judaea was constituted a Roman province.

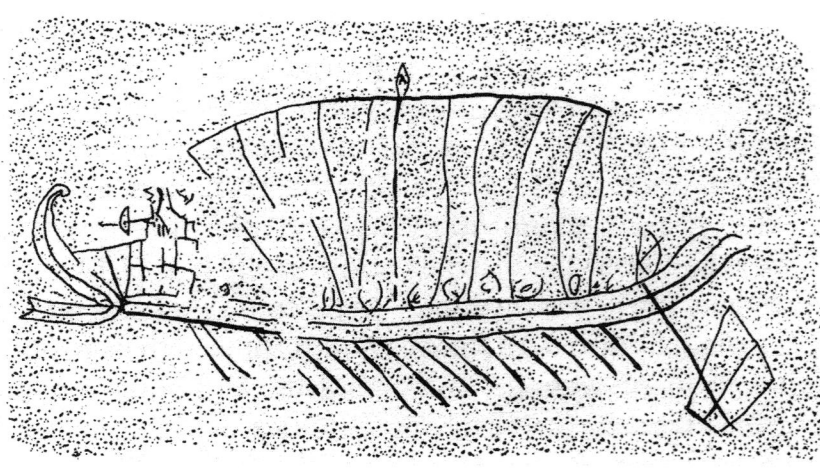

Warship on wall of Jason's Tomb, Jerusalem

There are few more fascinating stories in world history than the development of a group of hill settlements on the left bank of the Tiber, about 15 miles from its mouth, into a city which gradually dominated its immediate neighbors, then became mistress of Italy, survived an almost fatal conflict with Carthage, was drawn into the affairs of Greece, Asia Minor, Syria and Egypt and, by the middle of the first century B.C., ruled the Mediterranean world.

The Romans appear in biblical history at the beginning of the second century B.C. In 198 B.C. they declared a protectorate over the Greek city-states and, when the Seleucid king Antiochus III invaded Greece six years later, they drove him out and followed him into his own kingdom, where he was heavily defeated by a Roman general at the battle of Magnesia (190 B.C.). This general, Scipio Asiaticus, figures in Daniel 11:18 as the "commander" who put an end to Antiochus's "insolence." In the rivalry between the Ptolemies and the Seleucids Rome, from then on, took the Ptolemies' side. When Judas Maccabeus and his brothers revolted against the Seleucids in 167 B.C. and the following years, the Romans encouraged them.

In 133 B.C. the last king of Pergamum bequeathed his kingdom, which covered much of Western Asia Minor, to the Roman state; it became the Roman province of Asia. In 88 B.C. the king of Pontus (on the south shore of the Black Sea) expelled the Romans temporarily from Asia, but involved himself in a war with them that ended in his downfall twenty-five years later. By 63 B.C. the Romans found themselves obliged to reorganize the whole of Western Asia. Syria was constituted a Roman province;

ROMAN EMPIRE

Roman infantry officers

Roman warship

Captured Temple vessels; Arch of Titus, Rome

Judaea also became subject to Rome but for several decades continued to be governed by Jewish rulers, notably Herod the Great (37-4 B.C.) and his heirs.

After decades of civil war in Rome, Octavian (the adopted son of Julius Caesar) defeated the last of his rivals in 31 B.C. and speedily established his position as undisputed head of the Roman Empire, with the title Augustus. He organized the Empire from the English Channel to the Euphrates, making suitable provision for its defence. Those provinces which required the presence of a standing army were commanded by legates appointed directly by himself, like Quirinus in Syria (Luke 2:2). Augustus was commander-in-chief of all the Roman armies. Those provinces which were peaceful were governed by proconsuls appointed by the Roman senate, like Sergius Paulus in Cyprus (Acts 13:7) and Gallio in Achaia (Acts 18:12). So well organized was the empire that it survived periods of weakness and internal strife at the center, as at the assassination of the Emperor Gaius (A.D. 41) or the rise and fall of the three short-lived emperors between the death of Nero and the accession of Vespasian (A.D. 68-69).

Jesus was born at Bethlehem in Judaea, some six miles south of Jerusalem, shortly before Herod's death, but he spent most of his life in Galilee. He was brought up at Nazareth, about four miles southeast of Sepphoris, which was until about A.D. 20 the residence of Herod Antipas, tetrarch of Galilee. Later, Antipas built himself a new capital at Tiberias, on the southwestern shore of the lake of Galilee.

The traditional sites of Jesus's baptism in the Jordan and his temptation in the wilderness are near Jericho. When he began his public ministry, he set up his headquarters at Capernaum, a Galilean fishing town on the northwestern shore of the lake. Other towns which feature in the record of his Galilean ministry are Cana, Nain, Chorazin and Bethsaida (which lies east of the point where Jordan enters the lake from the north). When Herod Antipas, after his execution of John the Baptist, began to take an ominous interest in the activities of Jesus and his disciples, it was easy for them to sail across the lake and find refuge in the principality of his brother Philip. It was there that Jesus fed the multitudes and healed the Gadarene demoniac. It was in Philip's principality, too, near his capital Caesarea Philippi (modern Banyas) that Peter confessed Jesus to be the Messiah, a turning point in the gospel narrative.

Jesus paid several visits to Judaea, the direct road to which led through Samaria. His best-known experience in Samaria was his meeting with the woman of Sychar at Jacob's well, a well whose fresh water can be appreciated today (John 4:4-42).

When Jesus visited Judaea, he found himself in a Roman province governed (from A.D. 26 to 36) by the prefect Pontius Pilate. A mutilated inscription bearing his name was discovered at Caesarea in 1961. For his last visit to Judaea, Jesus appears to have traveled through Transjordan rather than Samaria, crossing the Jordan opposite Jericho. The road between Jericho and Jerusalem was the scene of the parable of the good Samaritan. Near the Jerusalem end of this road was the village of Bethany, where Jesus could count on the hospitality of his friends Martha, Mary and Lazarus.

It was Pontius Pilate who sentenced Jesus to death by crucifixion. The Via Dolorosa in Jerusalem marks the traditional line of Jesus's brief journey from Pilate's judgment-hall (possibly in the Antonia fortress) to Golgotha. Golgotha lay by the main road just outside a gate in the (second) north wall of the city; its site is covered by the Church of the Holy Sepulchre. There, on the third day, his tomb was found empty. In resurrection he appeared to his disciples at various places in Judah and Galilee. His ascension traditionally took place from the location on the Mount of Olives called Viri Galilaei.

Roman theater, Caesarea

Sidonian merchant ship, A.D. 2nd–3rd cent.

The map illustrates the narrative of Acts 1-12, covering a period of fifteen or sixteen years after the death and resurrection of Jesus (A.D. 30). To begin with, the main concentration of Jesus's disciples was the church of Jerusalem, although there were groups of disciples elsewhere, especially in Galilee and even as far north as Damascus. But about A.D. 33, a campaign of repression was launched by the authorities against the Hellenistic (Greek speaking) members of the Jerusalem church, some of whom expressed sentiments which seemed to threaten the sanctity of the temple. They were forced to leave Jerusalem, and dispersed in every direction. Some traveled southwest and probably before long crossed the Egyptian frontier and carried the good news to Alexandria and farther west to Cyrene. But their activity is unchronicled.

We are more fully informed about others, who preached the gospel and planted Christian cells in the plain of Sharon and along the Mediterranean seaboard from Gaza to Caesarea. Yet others evangelized the cities farther north, including the seaports of Phoenicia (Lebanon). The disciples in Damascus had their ranks augmented by refugees from Jerusalem, and it was while he was in pursuit of those refugees that Saul of Tarsus (Paul the Apostle) was converted to Christianity and became its most active propagator. After a brief mission among the Nabatean Arabs (east and south of Damascus), he visited the leaders of the Jerusalem church and then returned to his native Tarsus.

Meanwhile, the Hellenists who carried the gospel to the Phoenician cities continued their northward journey as far as Antioch in North Syria. There for the first time the gospel was preached to pagan Greeks. Many of these accepted the new faith and were incorporated in a mainly Gentile church. The apostles in Jerusalem sent Barnabas to direct this forward movement. He in turn fetched Paul from Tarsus to be his colleague in this work. About A.D. 46, news of a severe famine and food shortage in Judaea moved the converts in Antioch to send a gift of money for the relief of their fellow-Christians in Jerusalem. This set the pattern for the early practice of inter-church aid.

About A.D. 46 or 47, the church of Antioch released Barnabas and Paul for missionary work in Cyprus and Asia Minor. The churches of South Galatia in Pisidian Antioch, Iconium, Lystra and Derbe were founded at this time.

The growing influx of Gentiles into the church was seen as a threat by some Jewish Christians, and a meeting was convened at Jerusalem to consider whether special conditions should be laid down for the admission of Gentiles. It was decided that they should be admitted on the same terms as Jewish believers, but they were urged to observe certain food restrictions and the like which would make it easier for Jewish Christians to have social fellowship with them (to eat at the same table, for example).

Paul, apostle-in-chief to the Gentile world, then embarked on two great campaigns of evangelization: the first in Macedonia and Achaia (Greece) which resulted in the planting of churches in Philippi, Thessalonica, Beroea and Corinth, and the second in Ephesus. For nearly three years (A.D. 52-55) Paul stayed in this city, and so effectively did he and his colleagues prosecute their work that the whole province of Asia heard the gospel and churches were established in all its chief cities. At the end of this period Paul briefly revisited Macedonia and Achaia, and then sailed for Judaea. He was accompanied by a number of representative Gentile Christians who carried money from their respective churches as a gift to the Jerusalem church.

In Jerusalem, Paul was involved in a riot and was taken into custody by the Roman administration. He was sent to Rome to have his case heard by the emperor. His voyage there was interrupted by storm and shipwreck at Malta, where he spent the winter months of A.D. 59-60. In Rome he stayed for two years under house arrest, waiting for his case to come up for trial. His presence there was a great stimulus to the progress of the gospel in the capital. His execution was probably one incident in the persecution of Christians which broke out in the aftermath of the great fire of Rome (A.D. 64).

While Paul's career is documented fairly fully in the New Testament, there were other missionary enterprises among both Jews and Gentiles at whose course we can but guess. The gospel reached Rome, for example, long before any apostle visited the city. The map above illustrates the great expansion of Christianity in Mesopotamia and Iran, which in those days belonged to the Parthian empire. Between 170 and 180 there were Christian churches in and around Carthage, and also at Lyon and Vienne in the Rhone Valley, which had been evangelized from the province of Asia.

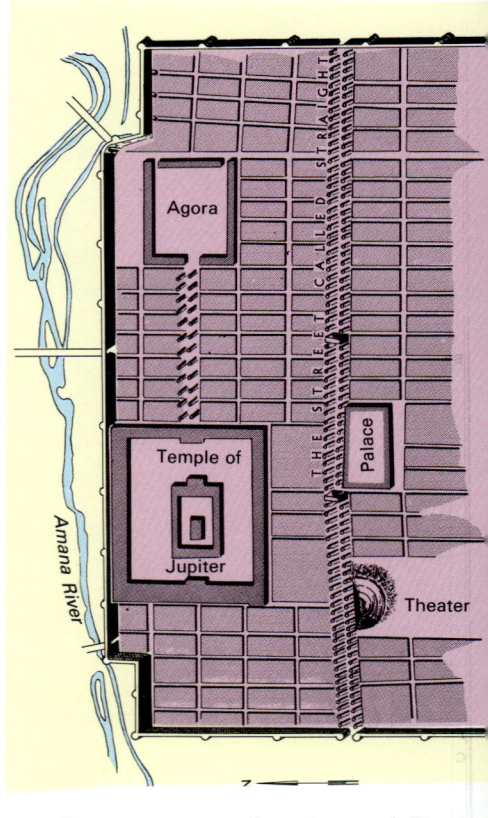

Damascus in the days of Paul

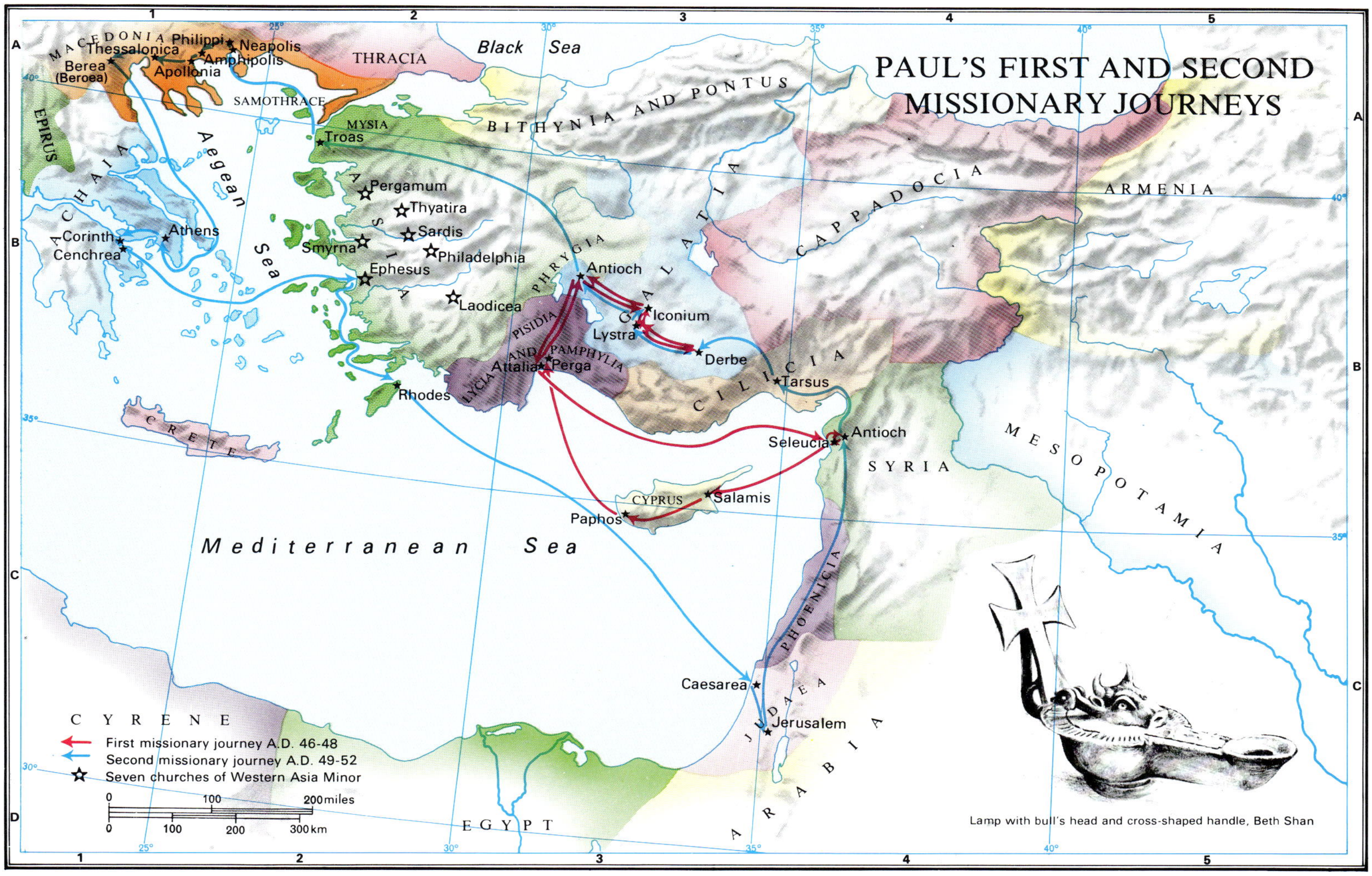
PAUL'S FIRST AND SECOND MISSIONARY JOURNEYS
MACEDONIA
Thessalonica
Philippi
Neapolis
Amphipolis
Apollonia
Berea (Beroea)
THRACIA
Black Sea
SAMOTHRACE
EPIRUS
ACHAIA
Aegean Sea
MYSIA
Troas
BITHYNIA AND PONTUS
Pergamum
Thyatira
Sardis
Smyrna
Philadelphia
Ephesus
Laodicea
ASIA
Corinth
Cenchrea
Athens
GALATIA
PHRYGIA
Antioch
Iconium
Lystra
Derbe
CAPPADOCIA
ARMENIA
PISIDIA
LYCIA AND PAMPHYLIA
Attalia
Perga
CILICIA
Tarsus
Rhodes
CRETE
Antioch
Seleucia
SYRIA
MESOPOTAMIA
CYPRUS
Salamis
Paphos
Mediterranean Sea
PHOENICIA
Caesarea
JUDAEA
Jerusalem
ARABIA
CYRENE
EGYPT
First missionary journey A.D. 46-48
Second missionary journey A.D. 49-52
Seven churches of Western Asia Minor
0 100 200 miles
0 100 200 300 km
Lamp with bull's head and cross-shaped handle, Beth Shan

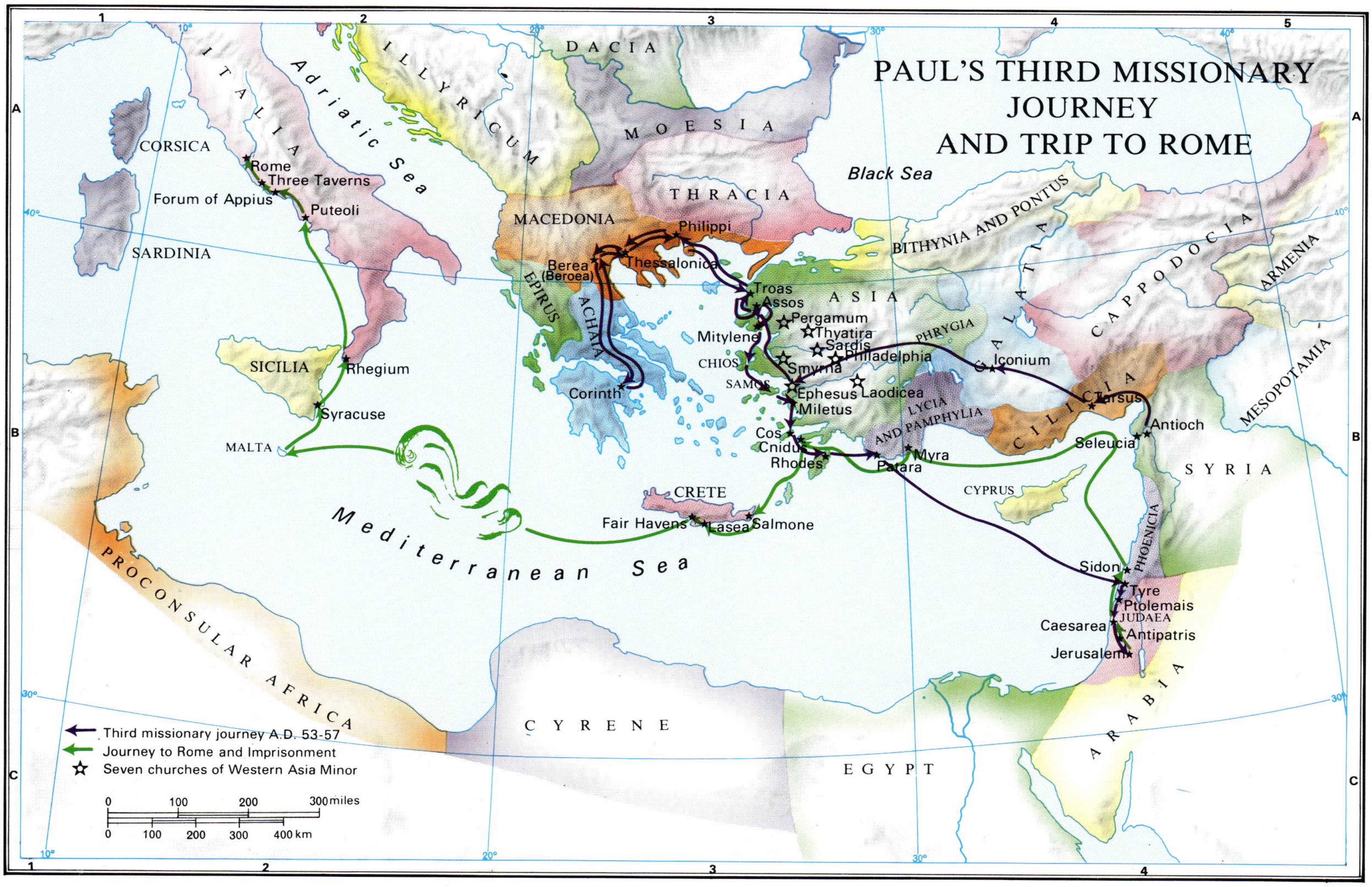
PAUL'S THIRD MISSIONARY JOURNEY AND TRIP TO ROME
CORSICA
ITALIA
Adriatic Sea
ILLYRICUM
DACIA
MOESIA
Black Sea
Rome
Three Taverns
Forum of Appius
Puteoli
SARDINIA
THRACIA
MACEDONIA
Philippi
Berea (Beroea)
Thessalonica
BITHYNIA AND PONTUS
EPIRUS
ACHAIA
Troas
Assos
ASIA
Pergamum
Thyatira
Sardis
Philadelphia
Mitylene
CHIOS
Smyrna
SAMOS
Ephesus
Laodicea
Miletus
PHRYGIA
GALATIA
Iconium
CAPPADOCIA
ARMENIA
MESOPOTAMIA
CILICIA
Tarsus
Antioch
Seleucia
SYRIA
LYCIA AND PAMPHYLIA
SICILIA
Rhegium
Syracuse
MALTA
Corinth
Cos
Cnidus
Rhodes
Patara
Myra
CRETE
CYPRUS
Fair Havens
Lasea
Salmone
Mediterranean Sea
Sidon
PHOENICIA
Tyre
Ptolemais
JUDAEA
Caesarea
Antipatris
Jerusalem
ARABIA
PROCONSULAR AFRICA
CYRENE
EGYPT
Third missionary journey A.D. 53-57
Journey to Rome and Imprisonment
Seven churches of Western Asia Minor
0 100 200 300 miles
0 100 200 300 400 km

Hagia Sophia, Constantinople

Roman coast guard ship, A.D. 2nd cent.

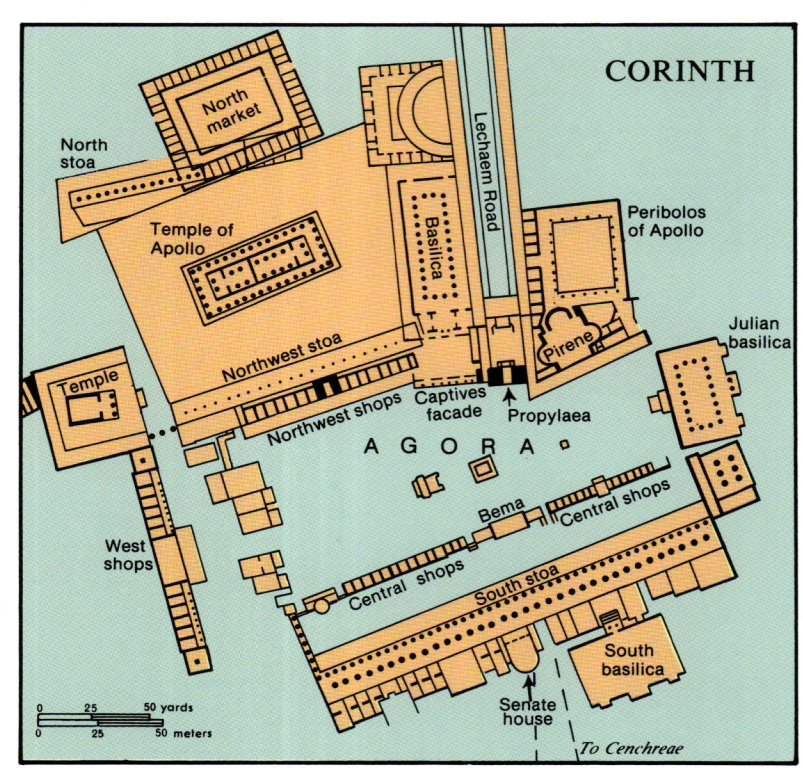

Christian victims in the arena

In the period illustrated in this map, Christianity was not only established in the regions shown, but secured the allegiance of rulers of various states including Edessa (modern Urfa), east of the Upper Euphrates (soon after A.D. 200), and Armenia (about A.D. 300). The Roman Empire first permitted Christians the free exercise of their religion in A.D. 313 (under Constantine); Christianity (orthodox Christianity at that) became the sole authorized religion of the empire under Theodosius (A.D. 381). How soon Christianity came to Britain is unknown; by 314 it was sufficiently well established for three British bishops (those of London, Lincoln and York) to attend a church council at Arelate (Arles) in the south of France.

The Syriac-speaking churches east of the Euphrates advanced the frontiers of Christianity down the Persian Gulf to the coast of India and overland through central Asia until in due course it penetrated China.

When Britain was invaded and occupied by barbarians from the continent (from A.D. 450 onward), these had to be evangelized in turn. Their evangelization was effected by two missions: a Roman mission in the south, led by Augustine of Canterbury (who arrived in 597), and an Irish mission in the north, led by Aidan, who came from Iona and settled in Lindisfarne in 635. (Ireland had been evangelized, mainly by Patrick, between 432 and 461; Iona was an outpost of Irish Christianity.) From christianized England the gospel was carried to Frisia and northwestern Germany.

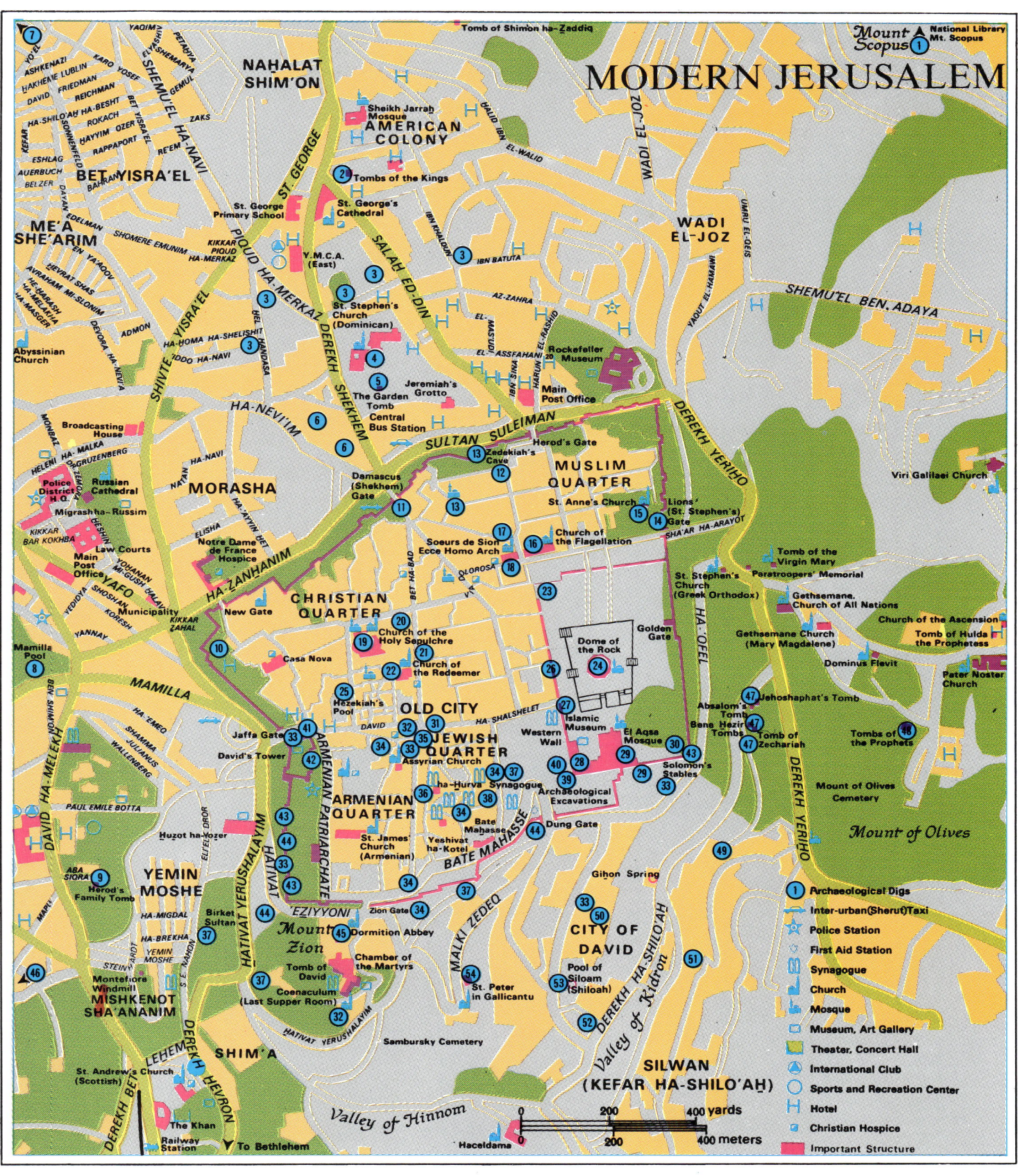

ARCHAE-
OLOGICAL
DIGS AND
REMAINS
FROM OLD
AND NEW
TESTAMENT
TIMES

1. Second Temple tombs
2. "Tomb of the Kings"
3. Remains of (Third) Wall
4. First Temple tombs
5. Garden Tomb
6. First Temple tombs
7. "Sanhedrin tombs"
8. Mamilla Pool
9. Tomb of Herod's family
10. Remains of (Third) Wall
11. Wall and gate, Second Temple
12. "Solomon's quarries"
13. "Zedekiah's Cave"
14. Sitti Maryam (Mary's) Pool
15. Sheep pools
16. Struthion Pools
17. First Temple tombs
18. "Ecce Homo Arch"
19. Second Temple tombs
20. Second Temple period wall
21. Second Temple period wall
22. Remains from First Temple period
23. Second Temple enclosure remains
24. Sacred Rock
25. "Hezekiah's Pool"
26. Warren's Gate
27. Wilson's Arch
28. Temple enclosure remains
29. Hulda Gates and Single Gate
30. "Solomon's Stables"
31. Hellenistic tower
32. Wall and gate, Second Temple period
33. Building, first Temple period
34. Building, Second Temple period
35. Israelite tower and building
36. Hezekiah's wall
37. Lower aqueduct
38. Building and pool
39. Robinson's Arch
40. Temple enclosure remains
41. Tower of Hippicus
42. Towers and building
43. Second Temple period walls
44. First Temple period tombs
45. Building ("House of Caiaphas")
46. Jason's Tomb
47. Tombs/monuments, "Absalom", Zachariah, Bene Hezir
48. "Tombs of the Prophets"
49. Gihon spring, Jebusite wall
50. First wall remains
51. Tomb of "Pharaoh's Daughter"
52. Siloam Pool
53. Second Temple period cisterns
54. Second temple period tombs

29

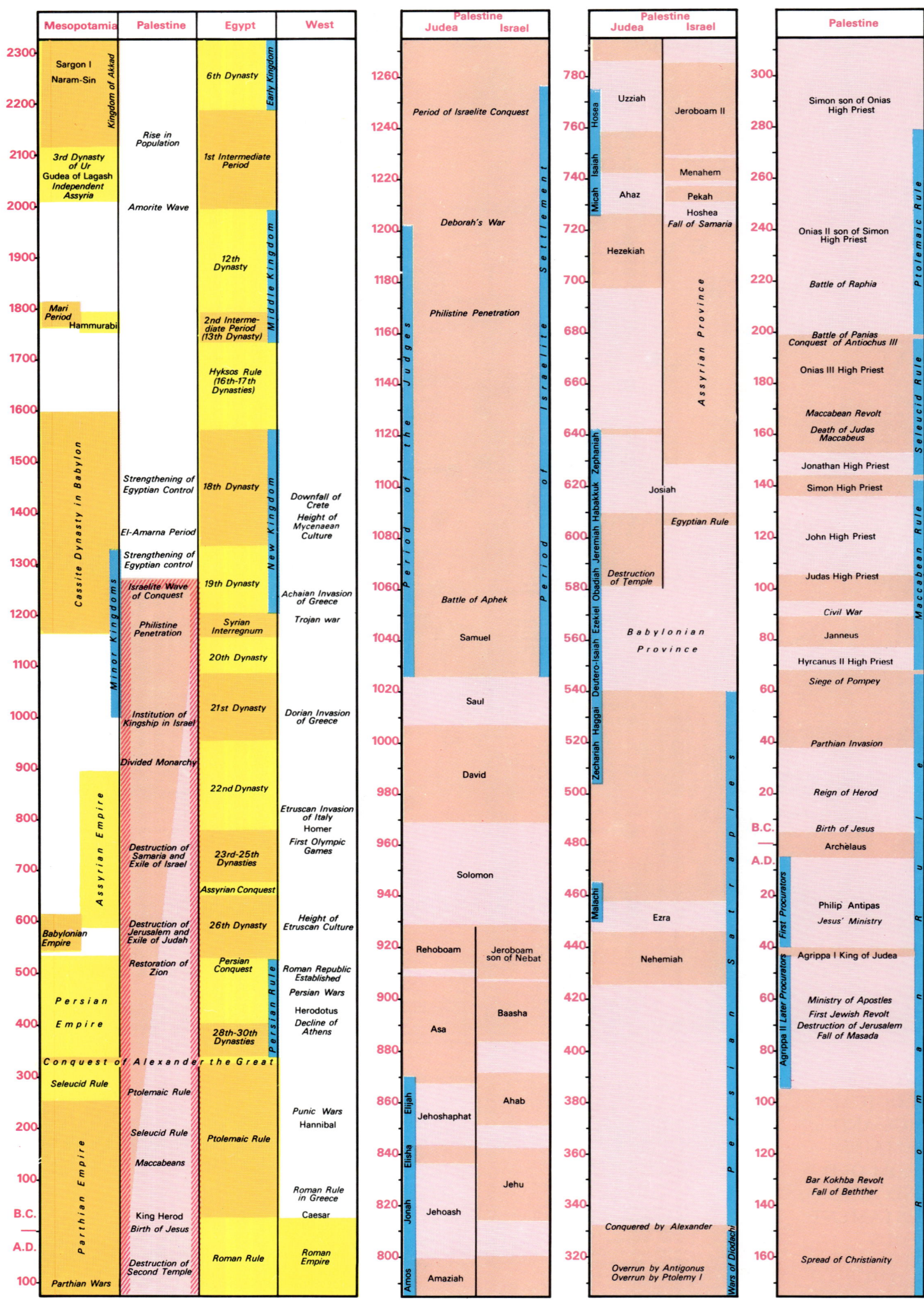

INDEX

* = Inset

A

Abdera (in Macedonia) 14 A4
Abdera (in S.E. Spain) 14 B1
Abdon, Judge 9 B2
Abila 17 B3; 21 B2
Abronah 8*
Abydos 14 A4
Acco (Akko) 11 C2; 28 B4
Achaia 18 B3; 24 B3; 25a B1; 25b B3
Achshaph 9 B2
Adiabene 24 B5
Adrianopolis 27 B3
Adriatic Sea 14 A3; 25b A2
Aegean Sea 14 B4; 25a B1
Aegina 27 B3
Aenos 14 A4
Africa 14 B2
Afula 28 B4
Agathe 14 E2
Ai 9 C2
Aijalon 11 D2
Akhetaton 4 D3
Akkad 6 C5
Alalakh 4 B4
Alalia 14 A2
Aleppo 4 B4; 6 B4
Alexandria 14 B4; 14*; 18 B3; 24 B3; 27 B4
Amastris 27 B4
Amisos 14 A5; 27 B4
Ammon 9 B2; 11 C3; 13 C3
Ammonium 14*
Amphipolis 25a A1
Anchialus 27 B3
Ancyra 24 B4
Anthedon 17 C2
Antioch (in Galatia) 25a B3
Antioch (in Pisidia) 24 B4
Antioch (Antiochia)(in Syria) 17 A3; 18 B4; 23 A1; 23*; 24 B4; 25a B4; 25b B4
Antiochia 17 A3
Antipatris 21 B1; 23 C1
Antonia Fortress 20
Apamea 23 B2; 27 B4
Aphek 9 B1; 11 C1; 13 C1
Apollonia 17 B2
Apollonia (in Cyrenaica) 14 B4
Apollonia (in Macedonia) 25a A1
Apollonia (in Thrace) 14 A4
Aqaba 28 E4
Aquae Sulis 18 A1
Aquileia 18 A2
Araba, Wadi 28*
Arabah 9 D2; 11 E2; 13 E2
Arabia 14*; 18 C4; 25a C4; 25b B4
Arad 8*; 9 C2; 11 D2; 13 D2; 28 C4
Aradus 23 B2
Aral Sea 14*
Aram-Damascus 11 B3; 13 B3
Arameans 6 B4
Arapkha 4 B5
Ararat, Mt. 28*
Arbela (Syria) 14*
Arelate 27 B2
Armenia 18 B4–B5; 25a A5; 25b B5
Armenians 27 B4
Arnon River 9 C2; 11 D2; 13 D2; 17 C3; 21 C2
Aroer 9 C2
Artaxata 18 B4
Arzawa 4 B2–B3
Ascalon (see Ashkelon) 17 C2; 21 C1
Ashdod 9 C1; 11 D1; 13 D1; 28 C3
Asher, tribe 9 A2
Ashkelon 9 C1; 11 D1; 13 D1
Ashqelon (Ashkelon) 28 C3
Ashtaroth 9 B2; 11 C2; 13 C2
Asia 24 B3; 25a B2; 25b B3
Asia Minor, Seven Churches of 25
Asochis 17 B3
Asshur 4 B5; 6 B5
Assos 24 B3; 25b B3
Assyria 4 C5; 6 B5; 18 B4–B5
Athens 6 B1 14 B4; 14*; 18 B3; 24 B3; 25a B1; 27 B3
Atlantic Ocean 17 A1–B1
Attalia 24 B3; 25a B3
Azekah 9 C1
Azotus (Ashdod) 17 C2; 21 C1; 23 D1

B

Babylon 4 C5; 6 C5; 6*; 14*
Babylonia 4 C5–C6
Bactra 14*
Baghdad 28*
Baptism, Site of 21 C2
Barak, Judge 9 B2
Barca 14 B4
Bashan 9 A2; 13 B3
Bat Yam 28 C3
Beersheba 9 C1; 11 D1; 13 D1; 17 C2; 21 C1; 28 C3
Beirut 28*
Benjamin, Gate of 10
Benjamin, tribe 9 C2
Beroea 24 A3; 25a A1; 25b A3; 27 B3
Berytus 23 C2
Bet-Guvrin 28 C3
Beth-horon 11 D2; 17 C3
Beth-shean 9 B2; 11 C2; 28 B4
Beth-shemesh 11 D2
Beth-zechariah 17 C3
Beth-zur 17 C3
Bethany 21 C2
Bethel 9 C2; 11 D2; 13 D2
Bethesda Pool 20
Bethlehem 9 C2; 17 C3; 21 C2
Bethsaida 21 B2
Betogabris 23 d1
Bezer (in Moab) 11 D2
Bint Jubail 28 A4
Bisher 8*
Bithynia 14 A5
Bithynia and Pontus 18 B4; 24 A4; 25a A3; 25b A4
Black Sea 4 A4; 6 A4; 14 A5; 14*; 18 B3; 24 A4; 25a A2; 25b A4; 27 B4
Bozrah 9 D2; 11 E2; 13 E2
Britannia 18 A1–A2
Brook of Egypt 11 D1
Brundisium 18 B3
Burdigala 18 A1
Byblos 4 C4; 11 B2; 13 A2; 14 B5
Byzantium 14 A4; 18 B3

C

Cabura 14*
Caesarea 21 B1; 24 B4; 25a C3; 25b B4; 27 B4
Caesarea Maritima 23*
Caesarea Philippi 21 A2
Caiaphas, House of 20
Cairo 28*
Cana 21 B2
Canaan 4 C3–C4; 8*
Capernaum 21 B2
Cappadocia 18 B4; 24 B4; 25a B4; 25b B4
Carales 14 B2; 24 B1
Carchemish 4 B4; 6 B4
Caria 14 B4
Carmel, Mt. 9 B2; 11 C2; 13 C2; 17 B2–B3
Cartenna 14 B2
Carthage 14 B3; 18 B2; 24 B2; 27 B2
Caspian Sea 6 A7; 14*; 28*
Caucasus Mts. 28*
Celts 14 A2
Cenchrea 25a B1
Cerasus 14 A5
Chalcedon 14 A4; 27 B3
Charax 14*
Chersonesos 14 A5
Chinnereth, Sea of 9 B2; 11 C2; 13 C2
Chios 14 B4; 25b B3
Chorazin 21 B2
Cilicia 14 B5; 18 B4; 24 B4; 25a B3; 25b B4
Citium 14 B5
Cnidus 25b B3
Colonia Agrippina 27 A2
Constantinople 27 B3
Copts 27 B3
Corduba 18 B1; 27 B1
Corinth 6 B1; 14 B4; 18 B3; 24 B3; 25a B1; 25b B3; 26
Corsica 25b A1
Cos 25b B3
Cotyora 14 A5
Crete 14 B4; 18 B3; 24 B3; 25a B1; 25b B3
Croton 14 B3
Ctesiphon 18 B4; 24 B5
Cyprus 4 B3; 14 B5; 15 B4; 24 B4; 25a B4; 25b B4; 28*
Cyrenaica 14 B4; 24 B3
Cyrene 6 C1; 14 B4; 18 B3; 24 B3; 25a C1; 25b C3; 27 B3
Cytorus 14 A5

D

Dacia 18 A3; 25b A3
Damascus 11 B3; 13 B3; 14 B5; 14*; 17 A4; 18 B4; 21 A3; 23 C2; 24 B4; 28*
Dan 9 A2; 11 B2; 13 B2
Dan, tribe 9 A2
Danube River 14 A4; 18 B3; 27 A2
Dead Sea 9 C2; 11 D2; 13 D2; 17 C3; 21 C2; 28 C4
Debir 9 C2; 11 D2
Deborah, Judge 9 B2
Decapolis 21 B2
Delphi 6 B1; 14 B4; 24 B3
Derbe 24 B4; 25a B3
Derbent 14*
Dhiban 28 C4
Di-zahab 8*
Dibon 11 D2; 13 D2
Dioscurias 14 A6
Dium 21 B2
Dophkah (Serabit el-Khadem) 8*
Dor 9 B1; 11 C1; 13 C1; 28 B3
Dora (Dor) 17 B2; 23 C1
Dora (on Euphrates) 24 B5
Doria 14 B4
Drapsaca 14*
Dura Europos 27 B4
Dur Sharrukin 6 B5

E

Eben-ezer 9 B1
Eburacum 18 A1; 27 A1
Ecbatana 6 C6; 14*
Edessa 27 B4
Edom 11 E2; 13 E2
Edrei 9 B3
Eglon 9 C1
Egypt 14 C5; 14*; 24 B4; 25a C3; 25b C4
Egyptian border fort 8*
Ehud, Judge 9 C2
Eilat 28 E3
Eilat, Gulf of 28 E3; 28*
Ekron 9 C1; 11 D1; 13 D1
Elam 4 C6; 6 C6
El Arish 28 C2
Elath (Ezion-geber) 8*; 11 F2; 13 F1
Elburz Mts. 28*
Eleusis 24 B3
El Faiyum 28*
El Jazira 28*
Elon, Judge 9 B2
Eltekeh 11 D1
Elusa 17 C2
Emmaus 17 C3; 21 C1
Emporiae 14 A2
En-gedi 13 D2
En-kerem 21 C2
En Gev 28 B4
Ephesus 6 B2; 18 B3; 24 B3; 25a B2; 25b B3; 27 B3
Ephraim, Gate of 10
Ephraim, tribe 9 B2
Epidamnos 14 A3
Epirus 14 A4; 25a B1; 25b B3
Erech 4 C6
Eshnunna 4 C5
Eshtemoa 11 D2
Etham 8*
Etruscans 14 A3
Et Tamad 28 E3
Euhesperides 14 B4
Euphrates River 4 B4–B5; 6 C5; 18 B4; 24 B5; 27 B4; 28*

F

Fair Havens 25b B3
Forum of Appius 25b A2

G

Gad, tribe 9 C2
Gadara (in Gilead) 17 B3; 21 B2; 23 C2
Gadara (in Spain) 14 B1
Gades 18 B1
Gadora 21 B2
Galatia 24 B4; 25a B3; 25b B4
Galilee 17 B3; 21 B2; 23 C2
Galilee, Sea of 21 B2; 28 B4
Gallia 18 A1–A2
Gath-rimmon 11 C1
Gath (of the Philistines) 9 C1; 11 D1; 13 D1
Gaugamela 14*
Gaza 4 C3; 6 C3; 8*; 9 C1; 11 D1; 13 D1; 14 B5; 17 C2; 21 C1; 23 D1; 28 C3
Geba 17 B3
Gedor 13 C2; 17 B3
Gentiles, Court of 20
Genua 18 B2
Gerar 9 C1; 11 D1
Gerasa 21 B2
Gergesa 21 B2
Geshur 9 B2
Gethsemane, Garden of 20
Gevulot 28 C3
Gezer 9 C1; 11 D1; 13 D1
Gibbethon 11 D1
Gibeon 9 C2; 11 D2
Gideon, Judge 9 B2
Gihon Spring 10
Gilboa, Mt. 9 B2
Gilead 9 B2; 11 C2
Gilgal 9 C2
Golashkerd 14*
Golgotha 20
Gordium 4 B3; 6 B3

Goshen 8*
Gozan 4 B4

H

Hadera 28 B3
Hadrumetum 14 B3
Haifa 28 B4
Halal, Mt 8*
Hall of Justice 10
Hamadan 24 B5
Hamath 4 B4
Hamath (Tiberias) 11 C2
Harran 4 B4
Hattusa 4 B3
Hazeroth 8*
Hazeva 28 D4
Hazor 4 C4; 9 A2; 11 C2; 13 B2
Hebron 9 C2; 11 D1; 13 D2; 17 C3; 21 C2; 28 C4
Heliopolis 14*
Helkath 11 C2
Heptapegon 21 B2
Heraclea 14 A5
Hermon, Mt. 9 A2; 11 B2; 13 B2; 17 A3
Herod Antipas, Palace of 20
Herzliya 28 B3
Heshbon 9 C2; 11 D2; 13 D2
Hibernia 18 A1
Hinnom Valley 10; 20
Hippicus, Tower of 20
Hippius 23 C2
Hipponium 14 B3
Hippo Regius 14 B2; 18 B2
Hippus 17 B3; 21 B2
Hispania 18 B1
Holy of Holies 10
Hurrians 4 C4–B5

I

Iberians 14 B1
Ibzan, Judge 9 C2
Iconium 24 B4; 25a B3; 25b B4
Idumea 17 C2–C3
Ijon 9 A2; 11 B2
Illyria (Illyricum) 14 A3
Illyricum 18 B3; 25b A2
Iol 14 B2
Ionia 14 B4
Ionian Sea 14 B3
Irbid 28 B4
Israel 6 C3–C4
Israel, Kingdom of 13 C2
Issachar, tribe 9 B2
Istros 14 A4
Italia (Italy) 18 B2; 24 A2; 25b A2
Iturea 17 A3

J

Jabbok River 9 B2; 17 B3; 21 B2
Jabesh-gilead 11 C2
Jacobites 27 B4
Jahzah 9 C2; 11 D2
Jair, judge 9 B2
Jamnia 17 C2; 21 C1; 23 d1
Jarash 28 B4
Jarmuth 9 C1
Jazer 11 D2
Jenin 28 B4
Jephtah, Judge 9 B2
Jericho 9 C2; 9*; 13 D2; 17 C3; 21 C2; 23 D1; 28 C4
Jerusalem 4 C4; 9 C2; 10; 11 D2; 13 D2; 14 B5; 14*; 17 C3; 17*; 18 B4; 20; 21 C2; 23 D1; 24 B4; 25a C4; 25b B4; 27 B4; 28 C4; 28*; 29
Jesus, Tomb of 20

31

Jezreel 13 C2
Jezreel Valley 13 C2
Jokneam 11 C2
Joppa 4 C3; 11 C1; 13 C1; 17 B2; 21 B1; 23 C1
Jordan 28 D4
Jordan River 9 B2; 11 C2; 13 C2; 17 B3; 21 B2; 23 C2; 28 B4; 28*
Jotbathah 8*
Judaea (Judea) 25a C4; 25b B4
Judah 6 C3–C4
Judah, Kingdom of 13 D1
Judah, tribe 9 C2
Judea 18 B4; 21 C2; 24 B4; 28 C4
Judgment Gate 20

K

Kadesh-barnea 8*; 9 D1; 11 E1; 13 E1
Kamon 9 B2
Kandahar 14*
Kanish 4 B4
Karak 28 C4
Karnaim 13 C3
Kedesh 4 C4; 9 A2; 11 B2; 13 B2
Kenath 11 C3
Kidron 17 C2
Kidron Valley 10; 20
Kir-haresheth 11 D2; 13 D2
Kir-moab 9 C2
Kishion 11 C2
Knossos 4 B2; 6 B2; 14 B4; 27 B3
Kuntilla 28 D3
Kuwait 28*

L

Lachish 9 C1; 13 D1
Lagash 4 C6
Lake Gennesaret 17 B3
Laodicea 25a B2; 25b B3; 27 B4
Larsa 4 C6; 6 C6
Lasea 24 B3; 25b B3
Last Supper, Place of 20
Lebanon 28 A4
Lebanon, Mt. 28*
Lebo (Lebo-hamath) 11 A3; 13 A3
Leptis (Leptis Magna) 14 B3
Leptis Magna 18 B2
Lesbos 14 B4
Libya 14 B4
Ligurians 14 A2
Lindos 6 B2
Lindum 27 A1
Litani River 9 A2; 11 A2; 13 B2; 17 A3; 21 A2; 23 C2
Londinium 27 A1
Lower City 20
Lugdunum 18 A2; 27 A2
Lutetia 18 A2
Lycia 14 B4; 24 B3
Lycia and Pamphylia 25a B3; 25a B4
Lydda 17 C2; 21 C1; Lydda 23 C1
Lydia 14 B4
Lystra 25a B3; 24 B4

M

Maalot 28 A4
Macedonia 14 A4; 14*; 18 B3; 24 A3; 25a A1; 25b A3
Macherus 21 C2
Magna Graecia 14 B3
Mahanaim 11 C2
Malta 25b B2
Manasseh, tribe 9 B2
Maracanda 14*
Mari 4 C5; 4*
Mariamne, Tower of 20
Marisa 17 C2
Masada 21 C2
Massaga 14*
 Massilia 14 A2; 27 B2

Massilia 18 B2
Mauretania 18 B1–B2
Medeba 17 C3; 28 C4
Medes 6 C6–C7
Mediolanum 18 A1
Mediterranean Sea 6 C2–C3; 9; 11; 13; 14; 14*; 17 B3; 18 B3; 21; 20; 23 B1–C1; 24; 25a C2; 25b B2; 27; 28*
Megiddo 4 C3; 9 B2; 11 C2; 13 C2
Melita 14 B3; 24 B2
Melitene 27 B4
Memphis 6 D3; 14 C5; 14*; 18 C4
Men, Court of 20
Mephaath 11 D2
Merom, Waters of 9 B2
Meshed 14*
Mesopotamia 18 B4–B5; 25b B4
Midian 8*
Migdol 8*
Miletus 14 B4
Mitanni 4 C4–B5
Mitylene 25b B3
Mitzpe Ramon 28 D3
Moab 9 C2; 11 D2; 13 D2
Modi'in 17 C2–C3
Moesia 18 B3; 25b A3
Motya 14 B3
Mycenae 4 B1
Myceneans 4 B1
Myra 25b B4
Mysia 14 B4; 25a A2

N

Nablus (Shechem) 28 B4
Nafud Desert 28*
Nahariya 28 A4
Nain 21 B2
Nakhl 28 E2
Naphtali, tribe 9 B2
Narbo 18 B2
Naucratis 14 B5
Nazareth 21 B2; 28 B4
Neapolis (in Italy) 14 A3; 18 B2
Nebo, Mt. 9 C2
Negeb (Negev) 9 C1; 11 D1; 13 E1; 28 C3
Nehardea 24 B5
Nemausus 18 B2
Netanya 28 B3
Nicaea 27 B4
Nicomedia 24 A3; 27 B4
Nicopolis 27 B3
Nicosia 28*
Nile River 4 D3; 8*; 18 C4
Nineveh 4 B5; 6 B5
Nippur 4 C6
Nisibis 14*; 24 B5; 27 B4
Nizzana 28 D3
No-amon 4 D3
Noph 4 D3; 8*
Noricum 18 A2–A3
North Sea 18 A2
Nuhasse 4 B4
Numidia 14 B2
Nuzi 4 B5

O

Odessos 14 A4
Olbia (in Scythia) 14 A5; 18 A4
Olbia (in S. France) 14 A2
Olea 14 B3
Olives, Mt. of 20
Olynthos 14 A4
On 4 C3; 8*
Ophel 10
Ophrah 9 B2
Orontes River 23 B2–A2
Othniel, Judge 9 C2

P

Palmyra 18 B4
Panias 17 A3
Pannonia 18 A3
Paphos 14 B5; 24 B4; 27 B4
Paran 8*

Parthia 18 B5; 24 B5
Patala 14*
Patara 25b B3; 24 B3
Pegae 17 B2
Pella (in Macedonia) 14*
Penuel 13 C2
Perea 17 C3–B3; 21 C2
Pergamum 18 B3; 24 B4; 25a B2; 25b B3; 27 B3
Perge 24 B4
Persepolis 14*
Persia 14*
Persian Gulf 4 D6–D7; 6 C6–C7; 28*
Phasael, Tower of 20
Phaselis (in Asia Minor) 14 B5
Phasis 14 A6
Phenagoria 14 A5
Philadelphia (in Asia Minor) 25a B2; 25b B3
Philadelphia (Rabbah) 17 C3; 21 C2
Philippi 24 A3; 25a A1; 25b A3; 27 B3
Philistines 11 D1; 13 D1
Philoteria 17 B3
Phocaea 14 B4
Phoenicia (Phoenicians) 6 C4; 11 B2; 13 B2; 17 A3; 23 C2; 25a C4; 25b B4
Phrygia (Phrygians) 14 B5; 18 B3; 24 B3; 25a B3; 25b B4
Pirathon 9 B2
Pisidia 24 B4; 25a B3
Pithom 8*
Ponticapaeum 14 A5; 18 A4
Pontic Mts. 28*
Pontus and Bithynia 24 A4
Potidaea 14 A4
Praetorium 20
Ptolemais (Acco) 14 B5; 17 B3; 21 B2; 23 C2; 24 B4; 25b B4
Pumbeditha 24 B5
Punon 9 D2
Pura 14*
Puteoli 24 A2; 25b A2; 27 B2

Q

Qatna 4 C4
Qiryat Gat 28 C3
Qiryat Shemona 28 A4
Qumran 21 C2; 21*
Quneitra 28 A4
Quseima 28 D3
Quzrin 28 A4

R

Rabbah (Philadelphia) 9 C2; 11 D2; 13 D2
Raetia 18 A2
Rafah 28 C3
Ramesses 8*
Ramoth-gilead 9 B2; 11 C2; 13 C2
Raphia 11 D1; 17 C2
Raphon 17 B4
Red Sea 4 D3–D4; 6 D3–D4; 11 F1; 14 C5; 14*; 24 C4; 27 C4; 28*
Regina Castra 18 A2
Rephidim 8*
Reuben, tribe 9 C2
Rhagae 14*
Rhegium 14 B3; 24 B2; 25b B2
Rhine River 18 A2
Rhinocorura 17 C1
Rhodes 14 B4; 24 B3; 25a B2; 25b B3
Robinson's Arch 20
Rome 14 A3; 18 B2; 18*; 24 A2; 25b A2; 27 B2
Royal Porch 20
Rumah 13 C2

S

Sabrata 14 B3
Safad 28 B4

Salamis 6 B3; 14 B5; 24 B4; 25a B3; 27 B4
Salmone 24 B3; 25b B3
Salonae 27 B3
Salt 28 B4
Samaria (city) 13 C2; 21 B2; 23 C2
Samaria (Palace of the Kings) 13*
Samaria (region) 17 B3; 21 B2; 28 B4
Samos 25b B3; 27 B3
Samosata 27 B4
Samothrace 25a A2
Samson, Judge 9 C1
Sardes (Sardis) 6 B2; 14*; 24 B3; 25a B2; 25b B3; 27 B3
Sardinia 24 A1; 25b A1
Sardis (see Sardes)
Sarmatia 18 A4
Scythia 14 A5
Scythopolis (see Beth-shean) 17 B3; 21 B2; 23 C2
Sede Boqer 28 D3
Sederot 28 C3
Sedom 28 C4
Seleucia 17 A3; 23 A1; 24 B4; 25a B4; 25b B4
Sepphoris 17 B3; 21 B2
Shamgar, Judge 9 B2
Shamir 9 B2
Sharon, Plain of 9 B1; 11 C1; 13 C1
Sharuhen 4 C3; 11 D1
Shatt al Arab 28*
Shaubak 28 D4
Shechem 9 B2; 11 C2; 13 C2; 17 B3; 28 B4
Sheep Gate 20
Shefaram 28 B4
Shiloh 9 B2; 11 C2
Shunat Nimrin 28 C4
Sicilia 25b B2
Sicily 14 B3; 24 B2
Side 14 B5
Sidon 4 C4; 6 C4; 11 B2; 13 B2; 14 B5; 17 A3; 21 A2; 23 C2; 24 B4; 25b B4
Simeon, tribe 9 C1
Sinai, Mt. 8*; 27 C4
Sinai, Peninsula 28 D2; 28*
Sinn, Mt. 8*
Sinope 14 A5; 24 A4; 27 B4
Sippar 4 C5
Sirhan, Wadi 28*
Smyrna 25a B2; 25b B3
Sparta 6 B1; 14 B4; 14*
Stoning of Stephen, Site of 20
Strato's Tower 17 B2
Succoth 8*
Succoth (in Jordan Valley) 13 C2
Susa 3 C6; 4 C6; 6 C6; 14*; 24 B5
Sybaris 14 B3
Sycaminum 11 D1
Sychar 21 B2
Syracuse 14 B3; 18 B3; 24 B2; 25b B2; 27 B3
Syria 14*; 18 B4; 23 B2; 24 B4; 25a B4; 25b B4
Syrian Desert 28*

T

Taanach 9 B2; 11 C2; 13 C2
Tabor, Mt. 9 B2; 17 B3; 21 B2
Tadmor 4 C4; 6 C4
Tafila 28 D4
Tamar 9 D2; 11 E2; 13 E2
Tanais 14 A5
Tarentum 14 A3
Taricheae 17 B3
Tarraco 18 B2
Tarsus 6 B3; 14 B5; 18 B4; 23 A1; 24 B4; 25a B3; 25b B4 27 B4
Tauchira 14 B4
Taurus Mts. 28*
Tel Aviv-Yafo 28 B3

Teman 13 E2
Temple 20
Temple Mount 20
Temptation, Mount of 21 C2
Tetrarchy of Philip 21 A2
Thapsacus 14*
Thapsus 14 B3
Tharros 14 B2
Thebes 6 D3; 14 C5
Thessalonica 18 B3; 24 A3; 25a A1; 25b A3
Thrace 14 A4; 18 B3; 24 A3
Thracia (Thrace) 25a A2; 25b A3
Three Taverns 25b A2
Thyatira 25a B2; 25b B3
Tiberias 21 B2; 23 C2; 28 B4
Tigris River 4 B5; 6 B5–C5; 18 B4–B5; 24 B5; 27 B5; 28*
Tingis 14 B1
Tipasa 14 B2
Tirqa 4 C5
Tirzah 13 C2
Tola, Judge 9 B2
Toletum 18 B1
Trapezos 14 A5
Tripolis 23 B2
Troas 25a B2; 25b B3
Troy 14 B4; 24 B3
Troy 4 B2
Tubas 28 B4
Tuttul 4 C5
Tyras 14 A5
Tyre 4 C4; 6 C4; 9 A2; 11 B2; 13 B2; 14 B5; 14*; 17 A3; 18 B4; 23 C2; 21 A2; 24 B4; 25b B4; 27 B4; 28 A4
Tyropoeon Valley 20
Tyrrhenian Sea 14 A3

U

Ugarit 4 B4
Ullaza 4 C4
Upper City 20
Ur 4 C6
Urartu 6 B5–B6
Urmia, Lake 28*
Utica 14 B3

V

Valley Gate 10
Van, Lake 28*
Vienna 18 A2; 27 A2
Vindobona (Vienna) 18 A3

W

Washshukanni 4 B5
Way of the Cross 20
Way of the Land of the Philistines 8*
Wilderness of Paran 8*
Wilson's Arch 20
Women, Court of 20

Y

Yafo 28 B3
Yam Hamelah (Dead Sea) 28 C4
Yarmuk River 9 B2; 11 C2; 13 C2; 17 B3; 21 B2
Yotvata 28 E4

Z

Zagros Mts. 28*
Zalmonah 9 D2
Zaphon 9 B2
Zarephath 13 B2
Zebulun, tribe 9 B2
Zered River 9 D2; 11 E2; 13 E2; 21 D2
Zikron Yaaqov 28 B3
Zin, Wilderness (Desert) of 9 D1
Zoan 4 C3; 8*
Zoar 9 C2; 17 C3
Zorah 9 C1